S0-BSP-329

(503) 644-0043

WITHDRAWN
CEDAR MILL LIBRARY

DRUG ADDICTION AND RECOVERY

Stimulants: Meth, Cocaine, and Amphetamines

DRUG ADDICTION AND RECOVERY

Stimulants: Meth, Cocaine, and Amphetamines

John Perritano

SERIES CONSULTANT

SARA BECKER, Ph.D.

Brown University School of Public Health
Warren Alpert Medical School

MASON CREST

Mason Crest
450 Parkway Drive, Suite D
Broomall, PA 19008
www.masoncrest.com

© 2017 by Mason Crest, an imprint of National Highlights, Inc. All rights reserved.
No part of this publication may be reproduced or transmitted in any form or by any
means, electronic or mechanical, including photocopying, recording, taping, or
any information storage and retrieval system, without permission from the publisher.

MTM Publishing, Inc.
www.mtmpublishing.com

President: Valerie Tomaselli
Vice President, Book Development: Hilary Poole
Designer: Annemarie Redmond
Copyeditor: Peter Jaskowiak
Editorial Assistant: Andrea St. Aubin

Series ISBN: 978-1-4222-3598-0
Hardback ISBN: 978-1-4222-3611-6
E-Book ISBN: 978-1-4222-8255-7

Cataloging-in-Publication Data on file with the Library of Congress

Printed and bound in the United States of America.

First printing
9 8 7 6 5 4 3 2 1

QR CODES AND LINKS TO THIRD PARTY CONTENT
You may gain access to certain third party content ("Third Party Sites") by scanning and using
the QR Codes that appear in this publication (the "QR Codes"). We do not operate or control in
any respect any information, products or services on such Third Party Sites linked to by us via
the QR Codes included in this publication and we assume no responsibility for any materials you
may access using the QR Codes. Your use of the QR Codes may be subject to terms, limitations,
or restrictions set forth in the applicable terms of use or otherwise established by the owners
of the Third Party Sites. Our linking to such Third Party Sites via the QR Codes does not imply an
endorsement or sponsorship of such Third Party Sites, or the information, products or services
offered on or through the Third Party Sites, nor does it imply an endorsement or sponsorship of this
publication by the owners of such Third Party Sites.

TABLE OF CONTENTS

Key Icons to Look for:

Words to Understand: These words with their easy-to-understand definitions will increase the reader's understanding of the text, while building vocabulary skills.

Sidebars: This boxed material within the main text allows readers to build knowledge, gain insights, explore possibilities, and broaden their perspectives by weaving together additional information to provide realistic and holistic perspectives.

Research Projects: Readers are pointed toward areas of further inquiry connected to each chapter. Suggestions are provided for projects that encourage deeper research and analysis.

Text-Dependent Questions: These questions send the reader back to the text for more careful attention to the evidence presented there.

Educational Videos: Readers can view videos by scanning our QR codes, providing them with additional educational content to supplement the text. Examples include news coverage, moments in history, speeches, iconic sports moments and much more!

Series Glossary of Key Terms: This back-of-the-book glossary contains terminology used throughout the series. Words found here increase the reader's ability to read and comprehend higher-level books and articles in this field.

SERIES INTRODUCTION

Many adolescents in the United States will experiment with alcohol or other drugs by time they finish high school. According to a 2014 study funded by the National Institute on Drug Abuse, about 27 percent of 8th graders have tried alcohol, 20 percent have tried drugs, and 13 percent have tried cigarettes. By 12th grade, these rates more than double: 66 percent of 12th graders have tried alcohol, 50 percent have tried drugs, and 35 percent have tried cigarettes.

Adolescents who use substances experience an increased risk of a wide range of negative consequences, including physical injury, family conflict, school truancy, legal problems, and sexually transmitted diseases. Higher rates of substance use are also associated with the leading causes of death in this age group: accidents, suicide, and violent crime. Relative to adults, adolescents who experiment with alcohol or other drugs progress more quickly to a full-blown substance use disorder and have more co-occurring mental health problems.

The National Survey on Drug Use and Health (NSDUH) estimated that in 2015 about 1.3 million adolescents between the ages of 12 and 17 (5 percent of adolescents in the United States) met the medical criteria for a substance use disorder. Unfortunately, the vast majority of these

IF YOU NEED HELP NOW . . .

SAMHSA's National Helpline provides referrals for mental-health or substance-use counseling.
1-800-662-HELP (4357) or https://findtreatment.samhsa.gov

SAMHSA's National Suicide Prevention Lifeline provides crisis counseling by phone or online, 24-hours-a-day and 7 days a week.
1-800-273-TALK (8255) or http://www.suicidepreventionlifeline.org

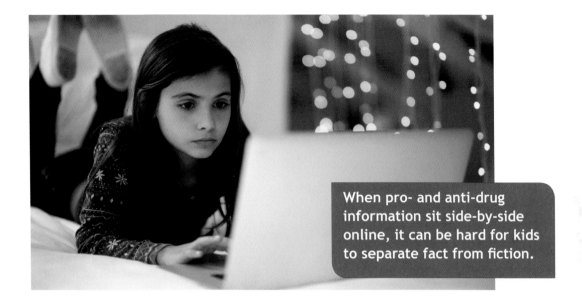

When pro- and anti-drug information sit side-by-side online, it can be hard for kids to separate fact from fiction.

adolescents did not receive treatment. Less than 10 percent of those with a diagnosis received specialty care, leaving 1.2 million adolescents with an unmet need for treatment.

The NSDUH asked the 1.2 million adolescents with untreated substance use disorders why they didn't receive specialty care. Over 95 percent said that they didn't think they needed it. The other 5 percent reported challenges finding quality treatment that was covered by their insurance. Very few treatment providers and agencies offer substance use treatment designed to meet the specific needs of adolescents. Meanwhile, numerous insurance plans have "opted out" of providing coverage for addiction treatment, while others have placed restrictions on what is covered.

Stigma about substance use is another serious problem. We don't call a person with an eating disorder a "food abuser," but we use terms like "drug abuser" to describe individuals with substance use disorders. Even treatment providers often unintentionally use judgmental words, such as describing urine screen results as either "clean" or "dirty." Underlying this language is the idea that a substance use disorder is some kind of moral failing or character flaw, and that people with these disorders deserve blame or punishment for their struggles.

And punish we do. A 2010 report by CASA Columbia found that in the United States, 65 percent of the 2.3 million people in prisons and jails met medical criteria for a substance use disorder, while another 20 percent had histories of substance use disorders, committed their crimes while under the influence of alcohol or drugs, or committed a substance-related crime. Many of these inmates spend decades in prison, but only 11 percent of them receive any treatment during their incarceration. Our society invests significantly more money in punishing individuals with substance use disorders than we do in treating them.

At a basic level, the ways our society approaches drugs and alcohol—declaring a "war on drugs," for example, or telling kids to "Just Say No!"—reflect a misunderstanding about the nature of addiction. The reality is that addiction is a disease that affects all types of people—parents and children, rich and poor, young and old. Substance use disorders stem from a complex interplay of genes, biology, and the environment, much like most physical and mental illnesses.

The way we talk about recovery, using phrases like "kick the habit" or "breaking free," also misses the mark. Substance use disorders are chronic, insidious, and debilitating illnesses. Fortunately, there are a number of effective treatments for substance use disorders. For many patients, however, the road is long and hard. Individuals recovering from substance use disorders can experience horrible withdrawal symptoms, and many will continue to struggle with cravings for alcohol or drugs. It can be a daily struggle to cope with these cravings and stay abstinent. A popular saying at Alcoholics Anonymous (AA) meetings is "one day at a time," because every day of recovery should be respected and celebrated.

There are a lot of incorrect stereotypes about individuals with substance use disorders, and there is a lot of false information about the substances, too. If you do an Internet search on the term "marijuana," for instance, two top hits are a web page by the National Institute on Drug Abuse and a page operated by Weedmaps, a medical and recreational marijuana dispensary. One of these pages publishes scientific information and one publishes pro-marijuana articles. Both pages have a high-quality, professional appearance. If you had never heard of either organization, it would be hard to know which to trust. It can be really difficult for the average person, much less the average teenager, to navigate these waters.

The topics covered in this series were specifically selected to be relevant to teenagers. About half of the volumes cover the types of drugs that they are most likely to hear about or to come in contact with. The other half cover important issues related to alcohol and other drug use (which we refer to as "drug use" in the titles for simplicity). These books cover topics such as the causes of drug use, the influence of drug use on the family, drug use and the legal system, drug use and mental health, and treatment options. Many teens will either have personal experience with these issues or will know someone who does.

This series was written to help young people get the facts about common drugs, substance use disorders, substance-related problems, and recovery. Accurate information can help adolescents to make better decisions. Students who are educated can help each other to better understand the risks and consequences of drug use. Facts also go a long way to reducing the stigma associated with substance use. We tend to fear or avoid things that we don't understand. Knowing the facts can make it easier to support each other. For students who know someone struggling with a substance use disorder, these books can also help them know what to expect. If they are worried about someone, or even about themselves, these books can help to provide some answers and a place to start.

—Sara J. Becker, Ph.D., Assistant Professor (Research), Center for Alcohol and Addictions Studies, Brown University School of Public Health, Assistant Professor (Research), Department of Psychiatry and Human Behavior, Brown University Medical School

WORDS TO UNDERSTAND

euphoria: feelings of extreme happiness.

neurotransmitter: a chemical that carries messages between nerve cells and between nerve cells and muscles.

panic attacks: sudden, overwhelming feelings of fear or anxiety that prevent a person from functioning.

paranoia: unreasonable suspicion of other people.

synthesize: to produce a new substance through various chemical processes.

tolerance: the state of needing more of a particular drug in order to achieve the same effect.

CHAPTER ONE

WHAT ARE STIMULANTS?

Samantha ("Sam") lived in a suburban dream world of manicured lawns, soccer games, and visits to the mall. Even the name of her town, Walnut Creek, conjured images of lazy Sundays and barbecues. The family had two boats and a large-screen TV to go along with their four-bedroom house. But Sam was not having any of that. She didn't want anything to do with her sister, her parents, or their middle-class life. As she later told the *San Francisco Chronicle*, she didn't fit in.

Sam took her first drink when she was 16. It was a beer, and she liked it. She smoked pot, too, and she liked that even more. She dabbled in cocaine, and a few weeks later snorted methamphetamine, also known as crystal meth. Sam remembers it clearly. She was at a friend's house with four girls. Each put a bit of meth up their nose. Then they put a bit more. Sam was hooked.

Someone mentioned meth was called "tweak," and Sam began "tweaking" every day. The drug made her happy. Sam had struggled with depression in the

Heavy users like Sam will get their drugs wherever they can.

past, and meth held her feelings of depression at bay. She had also struggled with her weight, and drugs helped her to lose weight quickly. She became more sociable. Life was good—or so it seemed. Reality soon set in, however. And when that happened, Sam's life spiraled out of control.

Sam changed. Her appearance became more ragged. Her weight dropped from 145 to 100 pounds and she started losing her hair. Her school work suffered and she often showed up late for class. She started fighting with family and friends. Her parents tried grounding her, but she just snuck out her bedroom window and continued to use drugs. Sam's drug use put a strain on her family—her mother was already exhausted by muscular dystrophy, and her dad started to drink heavily. At one point, the meth supply ran low, so Sam used amphetamines and smoked pot instead. A few months later, the meth was back, and Sam was back using it.

That month she smoked meth every day, and things went from bad to worse. Sam stole from her parents, using their money to buy drugs. When her father confronted her, she ran away. That night she stayed at a friend's house and smoked pipe after pipe until morning. When she came back, her dad sat her down and asked her if she wanted to get help. Sam thought about it—about the effects on her body, her family, her friends, and her schoolwork—and finally agreed.

HOW STIMULANTS WORK

Sam's drug use involved various types of stimulants. Stimulants are drugs that speed up activity in the brain and spinal cord; this causes the heart to beat faster and blood pressure to increase. People taking stimulants often feel more alert and energetic. Stimulants can be smoked, inhaled, or swallowed. The most commonly misused stimulants are meth, amphetamines, cocaine, and medications used to treat attention-deficit hyperactivity disorder (ADHD), a condition in which children have difficulty controlling their behavior.

Some stimulants, such as caffeine, have been a part of foods and beverages for thousands of years. Starting in the 19th century, stimulants were created in laboratories to treat ailments such asthma, obesity, neurological disorders, and many other illnesses. Today, they are one of the most misused drug categories. The United Nations Office on Drugs and Crime estimates that 24.7 million people across the globe misuse 500 metric tons (551 tons) of stimulants a year.

Once inside the body, stimulants affect the brain by enhancing the effects of several key **neurotransmitters**. Neurotransmitters are chemicals that allow billions of brain cells, called neurons, to communicate with each other. Stimulants especially enhance the effect of two neurotransmitters— dopamine and norepinephrine. Stimulants increase production of dopamine, the "feel good" neurotransmitter. It can make you feel wonderful when your body produces it. But too much dopamine can cause a person to become nervous or hallucinate. That's because the chemical affects how a person moves and thinks.

Norepinephrine works like adrenaline, which the body releases when a person gets excited, fearful, or angry. Norepinephrine narrows the body's blood vessels and increases blood pressure and sugar levels. It gives a person more energy.

Caffeine is a hugely popular stimulant drug. It's obviously much safer than a lot of the other stimulants discussed here, but it's still a drug.

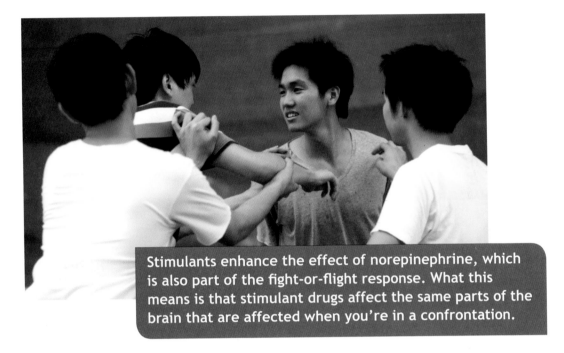

Stimulants enhance the effect of norepinephrine, which is also part of the fight-or-flight response. What this means is that stimulant drugs affect the same parts of the brain that are affected when you're in a confrontation.

TYPES OF STIMULANTS

Some stimulants are legal and have practical medical uses, although many are often misused. They include the following:

- **ADHD medication.** Adderall, Dexedrine, and Ritalin are all drugs prescribed to people suffering from ADHD. But people who don't have ADHD sometimes misuse these drugs because of their stimulant effects. For example, students in high school and college sometimes misuse the drugs so they can spend hours studying.

- **Caffeine.** Caffeine is a natural bitter substance found in tea, coffee, chocolate, kola nuts, and some cold medications. It stimulates the central nervous system, increasing a person's blood pressure, heart rate, and urine output. In small doses, caffeine is not usually harmful, and it can even have health benefits. But too much caffeine can make people jittery, restless, or have trouble sleeping.

- **Nicotine.** Highly addictive but legal, nicotine is found in cigarettes. Some research suggests that early nicotine exposure might lead to the

Nicotine is a highly addictive stimulant drug.

development of stimulant addiction. (For more on nicotine, see the volume *Alcohol and Tobacco* in this set.)

Other stimulants are illegal, and regulated by law. They include the following:

- **Cocaine.** One of the most-used illegal stimulants, "coke" or "blow" allows dopamine in the brain to build up in the gaps between neurons, known as synapses. When that happens, the drug overstimulates the neurons causing a temporary but powerful sense of euphoria. Like most stimulants, cocaine can increase a person's blood pressure and heart rate, which could lead to a heart attack. Regular use of the drug can also lead to paranoia, restlessness, irritability, and panic attacks.

- **Cathinones.** Another often-misused stimulant is synthetic cathinones, more famously known as "bath salts." Bath salts, which are not to be confused with what people put in their bath water to make it smell nice, are made illegally by street chemists using a variety of chemicals, including methylenedioxypyrovalerone, or MDPV, an amphetamine-like chemical.

- **Methamphetamine.** Also known as meth or crystal meth, the drug can be synthesized in home laboratories. Meth is highly addictive. Users can experience an exhilarated state of mind for hours. They can also have bouts of sleeplessness, a lack of appetite, and excess energy.

- **MDMA.** Also known as ecstasy, among other names, MDMA is a chemical compound called methylenedioxymethamphetamine. It is chemically similar to methamphetamine. Although classified as a stimulant, MDMA also has hallucinogenic effects, which allows people to see and hear things that aren't there. Some people believe that ecstasy allows people to emotionally bond with one another. Many people use the drug primarily for this feeling. (For more on MDMA, see the volume *Hallucinogens* in this set.)

BRAIN CHANGERS

Whether it's cocaine, meth, Adderall, bath salts, or some other type, stimulants are highly addictive because they affect the brain's pleasure centers. The more stimulants a person takes, the more pleasure they feel. The more pleasure they feel, the more they want the drug. Eventually, their bodies and their brains become dependent on the drug, because it inhibits the body's ability to produce its own dopamine. A person starts craving the drug and the pleasure it brings.

If they don't get their "fix," addicts will go through physical and mental withdrawal. Their bodies will shake. They will sweat. They will become

A man in Yemen chewing khat. Khat is a green shrub native to the Arabian Peninsula and East Africa that has strong stimulant properties. People chew the leaves, smoke them, brew them into tea, or sprinkle the leaves on food.

nervous, hostile, and paranoid. Addicts will build a **tolerance** to the drugs, requiring them to use more of it to get the same euphoric feelings.

BETTER DAYS FOR SAM

Back in the suburban enclave of Walnut Creek, Sam finally got healthy. She entered a drug treatment center and swore off speed and the other stimulants. She signed a contract with her parents. "Today is my last day using speed," it said. She made a list of her drug-using friends that she would no longer see. She agreed to submit to two drug tests a week.

But staying sober is easier said than done. Setbacks happen. Sam relapsed twice, which means she started using again. This is a common event for people with substance problems. But doctors treated Sam for depression and she got better. She set some goals and tried again. "I have goals and plans and deadlines and clean days to keep track of," she told a

BATH SALTS

Bath salts are highly potent, mind-altering drugs. They get a lot of media attention because of the extraordinary—and often horrible—things that people sometimes do when under their influence. In 2012 a Miami man who was high on bath salts tried to chew the face off another person; the attack only stopped after police shot him.

Bath salts were once sold legally in convenience stores and over the Internet. However, in 2012 the U.S. government made bath salts illegal to use, possess, or distribute. Bath salts can cause a variety of health issues, including panic attacks, hallucinations, delusions, paranoia, irritability, and violent behavior.

reporter. "I can use. I could die. Things will be the same if I use again. It used to solve problems when I was high. Now I deal with the problems. I don't want to go back."

TEXT-DEPENDENT QUESTIONS

1. What are some legal and illegal stimulants?
2. What does a neurotransmitter do?
3. What are three effects of taking bath salts?

RESEARCH PROJECT

Research the graphics found on the "Drug Facts: High School and Youth Trends" Web page, at http://www.drugabuse.gov/publications/drugfacts/high-school-youth-trends. Pick one of the graphics and write a paragraph or two describing the information presented and its importance.

WORDS TO UNDERSTAND

bona fide: genuine.

dilated: when the pupils of the eyes expand.

distill: to extract or remove.

launder: making money appear legal by passing it through legitimate businesses or bank accounts.

neurotoxicity: the poisoning of brain tissues caused by exposure to natural or human-made poisons.

psychotic: affected by a loss of contact with reality, marked by delusions and hallucinations.

CHAPTER TWO

METHAMPHETAMINE

Lori Kaye Arnold was a pioneer in the illicit methamphetamine business. Experts agree she was the person most responsible for providing addicts in the Midwest with a constant and cheap source of the drug. Arnold, the sister of actor Tom Arnold, had a multimillion-dollar meth operation in Iowa that flourished for a decade. It was easy for her to make the drug from readily available industrial and pharmaceutical ingredients.

Arnold got involved selling the drug out of necessity. She had dropped out of high school and began distributing meth to pay her living expenses. It was in the early 1970s, and many doctors prescribed the drug as a weight-loss aide and as an antidepressant. Arnold was one of those who struggled with depression, and when she took an illegal dose of meth for the first time, she felt better than she ever had. She knew making and selling the drug could yield big profits.

As the author Nick Reding writes in his best-seller *Methland: The Death and Life of an American Small Town,* Lori Kaye Arnold "was able to weave together [the] various political, sociological, and chemical threads into the Midwest's first and last bona fide crank empire. With [Arnold], the very concept of industrialized meth in rural places like Iowa was born."

Because of Arnold and many like her, meth became a cheap and easy way to get high. With names like crank, glass, ice, or crystal, about 10 million people tried the stimulant between 2005 and 2015. More than a million Americans reported using meth in 2012.

By 2001, Arnold was selling so much crank that she had to find ways to launder, or mask, the money she made so the police could not trace it back to her. She used her hometown of Ottumwa, Iowa, as her distribution center, eventually expanding into California and later into America's heartland. She perfected the cook-it-at home strategy, which cut down on costs and allowed her to become rich. But Arnold would ultimately serve 16 years in prison.

Law enforcement officials examine a package of methamphetamines that was seized southwest of San Diego, California, in 2014. The raid resulted in the seizure of more than 30 pounds of methamphetamines and approximately 3,500 pounds of marijuana.

METH'S INGREDIENTS

Either ephedrine or pseudoephedrine, which are found in many cough and cold medications, can be used as a key ingredient in meth. Because of this, the government has restricted their availability. Once meth is "cooked" by "chefs," it can turn into a white or brown crystalline powder. It can also turn into clear chunks that look like shards of glass. Cooks will also increase the strength of meth by adding battery acid, drain cleaner, lantern fuel, and antifreeze.

Meth is sometimes called "crystal" or "ice" because of its appearance.

THE HISTORY OF METH

The history of methamphetamine begins with the ephedra plant, which has grown in Pakistan, China, and the Americas for centuries. People in agrarian societies brewed tea from the ephedra plant and discovered that it relieved symptoms like congestion and coughing. By 1887, scientists were able to distill an amphetamine called ephedrine from the plant.

In 1919, Japanese scientists produced crystallized methamphetamine by combining ephedrine with iodine and red phosphorus. At the time, there

A German bomber photographed in a World War II reenactment. Many Nazi pilots used meth as a "pick-me-up."

was no single purpose for methamphetamine's use, although some people took the substance to treat depression or to lose weight.

It wasn't until World War II (1939-1945) that another use for crystal meth materialized. Pilots on all sides of the conflict used amphetamines to keep alert. But it was Adolf Hitler, the ruler of Nazi Germany, who was obsessed with the possibilities of methamphetamine. He and others saw the drug as a "pick-me-up" for tired pilots, tank drivers, and soldiers on the front lines. The Nazis manufactured millions of the tablets and distributed them to thousands of soldiers.

The Germans pills came in tubes with the name "Pervitin" embossed on the label. It was called an "alertness aid," to be taken "only from time to time." Some soldiers loved the "miracle pill" and couldn't get enough of it. One solider asked his parents to send him more Pervitin. "Perhaps you could obtain some more . . . for my supplies," he wrote. Taking the pill, he added, was like drinking liter upon liter of coffee. All his worries seemed to disappear, despite the horrors of combat.

The pills, however, were highly addictive. Soldiers would sweat profusely. Some died of heart failure. Others shot themselves during **psychotic** episodes. After the war, Pervitin was still easy to obtain. Doctors readily prescribed it as a way to curb appetites, or as a treatment for depression.

During the Cold War, a time of political and military tension between the Communist bloc, led by the Soviet Union, and the Western democracies, led by the United States, many soldiers in the armies of East and West Germany continued to pop the pills to remain alert. It wasn't until 1988 that Pervitin was banned in Germany, but the illegal manufacture of methamphetamine was just beginning.

BY THE BOOK

By the 1970s, motorcycle gangs on the West Coast of the United States had begun selling and distributing meth by distilling it from weight-loss medications. They set up makeshift drug labs where they made their own supply. In fact, during the 1980s and 1990s, biker gangs such as Hells Angels were responsible for 90 percent of the methamphetamine produced in the United States. The nickname "crank" actually came from the biker gangs, since bikers would hide meth in the crankcase of their motorcycles when they needed to travel long distances. When the bikers were producing meth, it was no longer in pill form, but crystallized. Yet only a handful of people knew how to make crystal meth, which contributed to high prices and limited supply. Then "Uncle Fester" came along.

Steve Preisler was a chemist living in Wisconsin. In 1984 he published a book that caused a sensation in the underground drug market. *The Secrets of Methamphetamine Manufacture* was a crystal meth cookbook. Using the pen name "Uncle Fester," a character on the old *Addams Family* television show, Preisler systematically outlined the process of converting ordinary drug-store ingredients into the mind-altering crystals. Police had jailed Preisler for meth possession earlier that year, two years after he graduated from Marquette University. While he was in prison, Preisler wrote his cookbook on a prison-issued typewriter.

"I was there with all the other cons [who were] mostly typing up court papers trying to appeal cases," Preisler said in a 2007 interview. "I did something a little bit more useful because appeals always get denied." The book explained how to create a lab and extract meth's main ingredients from cough and cold medicine, and then combine them with battery acid, antifreeze, or drain cleaner to increase potency.

As Uncle Fester's lessons spread, thousands of meth labs began springing up across the United States and around the world. People set

Meth in its powdered form.

METH TIMELINE

1919: Japanese scientists create methamphetamine in the laboratory.

1939-1945: Nazi and Japanese soldiers during World War II use meth while on duty to keep awake and alert.

1960s: Meth uses rises in the United States.

1965: U.S. government prohibits the possession, manufacture, and sale of various drugs, including amphetamines and methamphetamines.

1970s-1980s: Motorcycle gangs on the West Coast of the United States are responsible for producing 90 percent of the nation's methamphetamine supply.

1980: Phenyl-2-propanone, or P2P, the key chemical in amphetamine, is put under federal control.

1980s: Meth labs begin springing up along the West Coast.

1984: Steve Preisler, known as Uncle Fester, publishes *The Secrets of Methamphetamine Manufacture*.

1989: The Drug Enforcement Administration begins requiring companies that make 14 different chemicals used to make meth to keep sales records.

1990s: Meth cooks switch to cold medications as a source of ingredients because they are unregulated.

1998: Law enforcement officials say 80 percent of methamphetamine sold in the United States is controlled by Mexican drug cartels.

2005: Thirty-five states pass legislation restricting the sale of pseudoephedrine, while Congress says the drug has to be locked up in stores and users must register before purchasing.

2006: The United Nations reports there are 26 million meth addicts around the world. The United States has 1.4 million.

2014: The National Institute on Drug Abuse says 1 percent of 8th graders, 1.40 percent of 10th graders, and nearly 2 percent of 12th graders have tried methamphetamine at least once.

them up in bathrooms, basements, garages, hotel rooms, and cabins deep in the woods. Some people learned how to create meth labs in small suitcases, or in soda bottles.

In 2014 the U.S. Drug Enforcement Administration (DEA) reported that police had found 9,306 meth labs in the United States. Meth labs are dangerous places. They are packed with toxic, highly volatile chemicals. This makes meth labs vulnerable to explosions. The chemicals can seep into the environment when poured on the ground, the floor, or down the drain. As a result, groundwater sources can become contaminated. The labs also pollute the air as the meth is cooked. According to the U.S. Environmental Protection Agency (EPA), it takes between five and six pounds of toxic chemicals to create one pound of crystal meth.

Once crystal meth is made, users can snort, swallow, or inject it. One dose of contemporary meth is a thousand more potent than what Nazi soldiers used during World War II. Unlike many other drugs, meth creates a rapid, downward spiral that can alter a person's mind and impact their physical appearance.

HOW METH WORKS

Like other stimulants, methamphetamine affects dopamine in the brain, causing a person to become overstimulated with pleasure that can last all day. People can experience high levels of activity for hours. They'll act nervous. Anxious. They'll sweat. Their pupils will be **dilated**.

At some point, the drug wears off and the neurons don't create any additional dopamine. The pleasure begins to subside, and an addict then "crashes." When this happens, addicts may take more meth to continue the good feelings. These feelings can be so powerful that they will forget other things that gave them pleasure, such as eating, playing sports, or hanging out with friends.

Not only does meth affect dopamine, but it also affects serotonin and norepinephrine. Because of the effects on these neurotransmitters, a person will find it hard to fall asleep. Their blood pressure will increase and their heart will beat fast. The sudden rush of euphoria, the constant energy, the feelings of sexual prowess and desirability—these all keep a meth addict coming back for more.

PHYSICAL AND MENTAL CHANGES

Chronic meth use changes the chemistry of the human brain. Over time, it destroys the wiring in the brain's pleasure centers, making it hard to experience any joy at all. After a while, meth users can become violent, paranoid, aggressive, and confused.

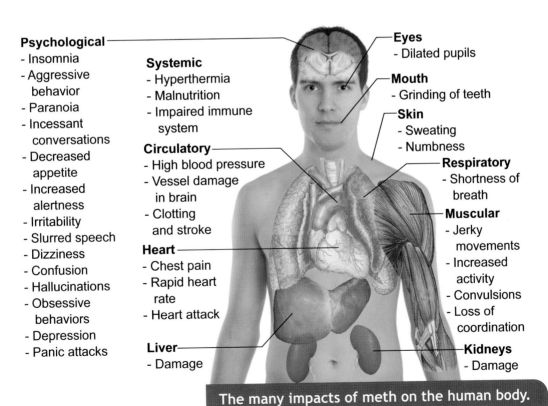

Psychological
- Insomnia
- Aggressive
  behavior
- Paranoia
- Incessant
  conversations
- Decreased
  appetite
- Increased
  alertness
- Irritability
- Slurred speech
- Dizziness
- Confusion
- Hallucinations
- Obsessive
  behaviors
- Depression
- Panic attacks

Systemic
- Hyperthermia
- Malnutrition
- Impaired immune
  system

Circulatory
- High blood pressure
- Vessel damage
  in brain
- Clotting
  and stroke

Heart
- Chest pain
- Rapid heart
  rate
- Heart attack

Liver
- Damage

Eyes
- Dilated pupils

Mouth
- Grinding of teeth

Skin
- Sweating
- Numbness

Respiratory
- Shortness of
  breath

Muscular
- Jerky
  movements
- Increased
  activity
- Convulsions
- Loss of
  coordination

Kidneys
- Damage

The many impacts of meth on the human body.

The most dangerous state of methamphetamine use occurs when a user has not slept in many days and becomes irritable and paranoid. This behavior is called "tweaking." When users "tweak," they become hyperactive and experience obsessive-compulsive behavior. People will do all types of bizarre things. They'll dumpster dive. They'll hallucinate. They might feel as if insects are crawling on their skin. They'll pick at their bodies and scratch themselves. They'll pick at their skin until they bleed.

Meth also takes a physical toll on the body. It destroys blood vessels, making it hard for the body to repair itself. Sores can appear and take a long time to heal. A person's skin can lose its luster. Teeth will often fall out as the chemicals eat through the enamel, the hard outer coating. The slang term for this is "meth mouth."

"Ms. Crystal Methamphetamine! That was my girl." So writes Jessica, who at the age of 14 had become a full-fledged meth addict. "I was in love with the pipe," she says. "I ran away, lived on the streets. I lost most of my friends because they quit talking to me because I was a tweaker. Crystal meth . . . is my worst enemy, but she's also my good friend. I'm only 17 and this is not right."

KICKING METH

Kicking the meth habit is difficult. Although some medications are effective in treating some substance use disorders, this is not true for meth addiction. No specific medications can counter the effects of methamphetamine dependence.

The first thing a meth addict has to do is to detoxify, or rid their body of the drug. Detoxifying can be a physical and emotional experience. Chronic meth use have wreaks havoc on the body as it depletes the levels of dopamine and other neurotransmitters. Repeated meth use can also cause **neurotoxicity**, which can result in brain damage. Consequently,

A key ingredient in meth-making is anhydrous ammonia, which is a common farm fertilizer. In Iowa, where the ingredient is stored in tanks all over the state, the government gives out special locks to help farmers keep their supplies safe from meth cooks.

it will take time for the brain to heal itself. A person detoxifying might develop depression, or become irritable, paranoid, or begin to hallucinate. The process can be dangerous and unpleasant. People often check into a residential detoxification center, which provides medical and psychological support.

Once the drug is out of a person's system, psychological work begins. Intense cognitive-behavioral therapy, which seeks to change a person's pattern of thinking or behavior, has proved useful in treating meth addicts and getting them off the drug. One of the most effective treatments is the so-called Matrix Model. The Matrix Model is a 16-week treatment approach that uses individual and family counseling, drug testing, and a 12-step support structure.

COMMUNITY IMPACT

Meth use does not just affect an individual person or his or her family. The presence of meth in a community increases crime, unemployment, child abuse, and other social ills. The labs where meth is made can easily burn down or explode, leaving a toxic mess in the neighborhood. According to a 2009 report from the RAND Corporation, methamphetamine use cost the United States $23.4 billion in 2005.

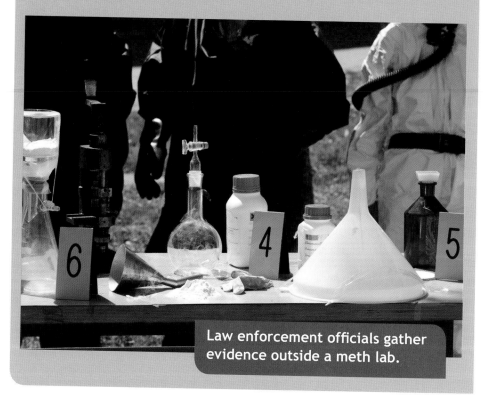

Law enforcement officials gather evidence outside a meth lab.

The goals of therapy are to identify and try to correct problem behaviors, as well as the negative thought patterns that led to these behaviors. Therapy helps users look at the negative consequences of their drug use, and to learn how to recognize cravings early and find ways to cope with them. Therapy also helps them learn how to avoid situations where drug use might present itself.

TEXT-DEPENDENT QUESTIONS

1. In what year did scientists first extract an amphetamine from the ephedra plant?
2. Who is "Uncle Fester," and why is he important in the meth trade?
3. What does the term "tweak" mean?

RESEARCH PROJECT

At the website of the Drug Enforcement Administration, you can find maps showing the number of meth labs that law enforcement found from 2010 to 2014 (http://www.dea.gov/resource-center/meth-lab-maps.shtml). Look at the maps for 2010 and 2014 and figure out the percentage of increase (or decrease) in the number of labs for each state. Next, print out a line map of the United States and put in the percentage for each state. Which states had the highest increase in meth labs? Which states had the lowest? Which region led the United States in meth production? What can you conclude?

WORDS TO UNDERSTAND

abstinence: the conscious avoidance of a certain behavior.

anecdotal: based on word-of-mouth stories rather than firsthand knowledge.

anesthetic: a drug that acts on the central nervous system and reduces sensitivity to pain.

freebase: the preparation of cocaine for smoking by heating it with water and a volatile liquid.

medicinal: able to treat an illness.

psychoanalyst: a therapist who treats mental health functions on both the unconscious and conscious levels.

CHAPTER THREE

COCAINE AND CRACK

Lower Manhattan is the world's financial heart, where fortunes are won and lost, and billions of dollars changes hands. Bond traders, bankers, and stockbrokers crowd the Wall Street area—courting clients, making deals, and either enriching or ruining their lives. Grueling workdays and juggling billions of dollars can create unbearable stress. Over the years, some people in the financial field have turned to cocaine to alleviate some of that stress.

Back in the 1980s, the image of Wall Street brokers snorting lines of cocaine off glass tables was a trite stereotype brought to life by Hollywood and dozens of memoirs. Yet, from anecdotal evidence provided by Wall Street insiders, cocaine is still widely used today.

"They have the disposable income. They have lives, which are often responding to the next crisis. They have access to drugs, drug-using friends, and associates, and they feel that drugs are part of the spectrum of entitlement," Dr. Mark Gold, from the University of Florida College of Medicine, told a reporter. "Wharton [School of Business] may have

The floor of the New York Stock Exchange. Stimulant use is common in high-stress environments like stock trading.

prepared them for [Wall Street], but they are not prepared by evolution or experience for cocaine . . . or other potent drugs of abuse."

ONE DRUG, TWO COMMUNITIES

The scene is much different 11 miles away in Harlem. There people also use cocaine, but for different reasons and in a different form. On one night in 2014, police arrested 19 people for selling crack, a crystallized form of cocaine that is significantly less expensive. Those who were arrested sold the drug in lobbies, hallways, elevators, and playgrounds of an East Harlem public housing complex. The ages of those arrested spanned from 18 to 38. Most were gang members.

Regardless of whether it is a powder or a rock, cocaine is addictive. In 2013 there were 1.5 million cocaine users 12 years old or older, making it the third most-used illegal drug in the United States. But although powdered cocaine and crack are identical on a chemical level, in real life the difference between the two drugs is stark. Depending on its quality and other factors, powdered cocaine can cost a person in upstate New York $50 to $120 a gram. Crack costs far less.

Cocaine powder is a glamour drug, used by socialites, celebrities, college kids, and anyone with a wallet full of cash. Crack, on the other hand, is anything but trendy. The drug has often been used as a scapegoat for a variety of social ills plaguing poor neighborhoods. It is comparatively cheap—both easy to make and easy to get. Since the 1980s, the so-called crack epidemic has been blamed for poor education, violence, and homelessness.

Despite the impression you might get from the media, cocaine is a much larger problem than crack in the United States. The U.S. National Survey on Drug Use and Health reported in 2013 that 14.3 percent of individuals aged

Crack is not just an issue in the United States. Here, a user in Brazil smokes crack using a tin can instead of a pipe.

12 and older said they had used cocaine, while only 3.4 percent had used crack. Yet crack users are more likely to be arrested multiple times, and they are more likely to face prolonged jail sentences. Many critics argue that sentencing laws unfairly target the poor and racial or ethnic minority groups, who cannot afford cocaine in its more expensive powder form.

Congress passed the Fair Sentencing Act of 2010 in order to reduce sentencing disparities. Before the act was signed into law, a person possessing 1 gram of crack would serve the same amount of time in jail as a person possessing 100 grams of powder cocaine. Under the new rules, 1 gram of crack will get a person the same jail time as 18 grams of powder cocaine.

COCAINE: A BRIEF AND BIZARRE HISTORY

Some 4,000 years ago, Native Americans living in Colombia, Peru, and Bolivia discovered the medicinal qualities of the coca plant that grew in the rain forests, reaching a height of nearly 18 feet. They harvested its leaves four times a year. They would then chew the leaves, which made them feel good.

Coca plants in the Andes Mountains, Bolivia.

It not only altered their moods, but it also helped them digest food and suppress their appetites.

When the Spanish came to South America in the 1500s, they found the coca plant and brought it back to Spain. From there, coca leaves spread through the rest of Europe. The Spanish, who came to the New World looking for gold and silver, enslaved thousands of Native Americans and forced them to work in these mineral mines. The Spanish kept the laborers supplied with coca leaves because it made the workers easier to control.

An advertisement from around 1916. Hall's Coca Wine used cocaine as a key ingredient.

It wasn't until 1859 that a German chemist named Albert Niemann found a way to extract the active substance in coca leaves. He called it cocaine. It was first used as a local anesthetic in eye surgery. Doctors then began experimenting with the drug. The famed psychoanalyst Sigmund Freud used the drug as a cure for depression and sexual problems. He called it a magical substance and used it himself.

In 1886 cocaine became a prime ingredient in one of the most popular soft drinks of all time—Coca-Cola. People who drank Coke testified about its energizing effects. *"Tired? Then Drink Coca-Cola,"* one advertisement of the period extolled. *"It Relieves Exhaustion. . . . You will be surprised how quickly it will ease the Tired Brain—soothe the Rattled Nerves and restore Wasted Energy to Both Mind and Body."*

When newspapers began linking cocaine to an uptick in crime, Coca-Cola stopped using the drug as an ingredient. Soon, people began trying new ways to get cocaine in their bodies—like snorting or injecting dissolved cocaine. Snorting allowed powder cocaine to be absorbed through the nasal tissue, which was a quick way for it to enter the bloodstream.

By the 1970s cocaine had become a fashionable drug. Entertainers, sports celebrities, and business people created a brisk business for cocaine dealers. It wasn't cheap, and as a result, cocaine became associated with the wealthy. By the late 1970s and early 1980s, cocaine had flooded the U.S. market. Adhering to the laws of supply and demand, the price dropped. Drug dealers then began converting cocaine powder into small chunks, or "rocks," known as crack. Drug dealers used baking soda (sodium bicarbonate) or sodium hydroxide to change the powder cocaine into rocks.

Users then **freebased**, or heated the rock crystal, producing a smoky vapor. A person inhales the vapor using a crack pipe. The term "crack" refers to the splitting sound the crystal makes as it is heated.

EPIDEMIC?

Crack, which is more potent and more addictive than powdered cocaine, was easy to manufacture and highly profitable. The drug spread across the nation, and ultimately the world. Most of those who used crack lived in large cities, and the drug became associated with the poor. Fueling this view was a research study claiming that "crack babies," children born to crack-addicted mothers, were doomed to an unhealthy future.

But in 2013, researchers found that cocaine exposure in the womb does not impact unborn children as intensely as the original study claimed. According to Dr. Deborah Frank of Boston University, the effects of cocaine use on a fetus are along the same lines as the effects of cigarettes—babies tend to be smaller and may be born prematurely. To be clear, pregnant women should never smoke or use cocaine. However, this idea of a generation of doomed "crack babies" is a myth. As Dr. Frank told the *New York Times*, "cocaine use in pregnancy has been treated as a moral issue rather than a health problem."

PHYSICAL EFFECTS

In addition to being addictive, cocaine affects the body in many ways. Here's a few:

- **Heart.** Cocaine increases heart rate, restricts blood flow, and increases blood pressure. It can also make your heart beat abnormally.
- **Brain.** Cocaine constricts the blood vessels in the brain, which can cause a stroke even in young people. It can also lead to violent or strange behavior.
- **Lungs.** Snorting coke damages the nose and sinuses. Smoking crack can irritate the lungs.
- **Kidneys.** Cocaine might cause your kidneys to fail, or at the very least cause kidney damage.

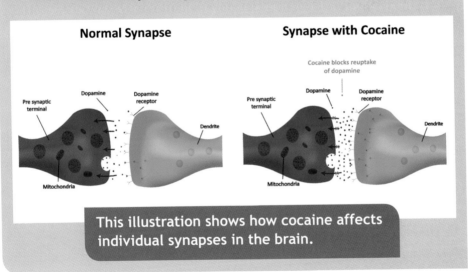

This illustration shows how cocaine affects individual synapses in the brain.

UPPER-CLASS CRACK USE

Crack is often seen as a drug for the poor, but Shane Schleger did not fit that profile. He was 21 when he learned to cook and smoke crack in a swanky hotel room in New York City. He was in town for a concert, and one of his friends showed him how to make cocaine powder into a rock. "These upper-middle-class suburban kids seemed to know every detail about the drug, from the minutiae of proper pipe handling . . . to the kinder, gentler euphemism for crack, 'hubbas,'" Schleger wrote on Slate.com.

Schleger smoked crack and liked it. He used it every day for three months. Then he stopped. And then he started up again, often bingeing on the drug. He still uses, but has stopped bingeing. "I'm not particularly interested in 'bottoming out' or destroying my life in exchange for whatever temporary benefit I get from smoking cocaine," Schleger admitted. "On the other hand, the path I've taken over the last 15 years indicates that I'm not motivated to achieve total **abstinence**. That's why I have tried to find a middle way, hopefully reducing the amount of harm I inflict upon myself."

Schleger admits he has a problem. He knows what smoking crack does to his lungs. He is aware of his "irrational paranoia, the unfounded fear that someone is out there monitoring my behavior." Yet he can't resist his cravings for crack cocaine. This is a common phenomenon among users, who initially start using to feel good, but eventually find themselves needing to use just to feel normal. "Despite my awareness that the drug has toxic physical and mental side effects that I want to avoid, past experience indicates that I will likely indulge my habit in the coming months," said Schleger.

HIGHLY ADDICTIVE

Schleger knows the consequences of crack use, and yet he still keeps using. That's because cocaine is one of the most addictive drugs there is.

Cocaine, like all stimulants, targets the central nervous system by increasing dopamine levels. In the brain of a normal person, when something pleasurable happens, such as eating a piece of cake or scoring the winning run in a baseball game, neurons release dopamine into the small space that separates two neurons—the synapse. Dopamine is then recycled back into the cell that released the chemical. Cocaine stops that process, forcing dopamine to build up in the synapse. The deluge of dopamine impacts the brain's normal function. The excess dopamine is the reason why a person gets high on cocaine.

The drug can have a powerful hold over people. Users will build up a tolerance to the drug, forcing them to use more to achieve the same pleasure. Many people binge on cocaine, using the drug repeatedly in a short period. They do this to sustain the high they experience. Cocaine increases a person's energy, elevates their mood, and provides a general euphoric feeling

In 2013, 1.5 million people aged 12 or older reported using cocaine. Moreover, 1 in 40 adults reported using it in the previous year. Males aged 18 to 25 use the most cocaine, with 8 percent reporting use over the previous 12 months.

A U.S. Coast Guard Law Enforcement Detachment prepares an estimated $78 million of confiscated cocaine from a drug bust made on August 16, 2013.

CAUSE OF DEATH

Len Bias was an outstanding basketball player with his future on the court settled. A standout all-American with the University of Maryland, Bias was the second player picked by in the first round of the NBA draft in 1986, when he was chosen by the Boston Celtics. Anyone who followed basketball back then knew the Celtics had gotten a gem of a player.

Then suddenly, at the age of 22, Bias was dead. He used cocaine and died of a heart attack in his dorm room long before he put on a Celtics' jersey. Bias was fit and healthy except for the massive amount of cocaine in his system. Unfortunately, heart attacks are one of the most dangerous side effects of cocaine. Other effects of cocaine include:

- loss of appetite
- difficulty sleeping
- high blood pressure
- respiratory failure (if smoked)
- weight loss
- malnutrition
- tooth decay
- depression
- reproductive organ damage in women

GETTING HELP

Cocaine parties. Barbara went to them all the time. They were fun, and her friends were there. Lines of coke were lined up on a table just waiting to be snorted. The drug made her feel strong, confident, and upbeat. The parties put her in a good mood at first. But soon bad things began to happen. She became addicted. She lost her best friend. She ended two relationships. Cocaine had taken hold of her life and wasn't letting go. Finally, she called a crisis hotline and got into treatment.

Nearly 13 percent of all people who seek drug treatment enter a program because they are addicted to cocaine. In many cases, they use other drugs as well. The treatment of choice for most people with cocaine problems is behavioral therapy, a type of therapy in which the therapist helps the patient to change potentially destructive behavior patterns. One type of behavioral therapy is called "motivational incentives," which helps increase people's motivation to change by rewarding them for specific milestones, like attending sessions, passing urine tests, or cutting down their use of the drug. They earn points or chips, which they can then cash in for items such as gym memberships, dinners, or movie tickets.

Cognitive-behavioral therapy (CBT) is another popular behavioral therapy approach. CBT helps a person to understand and identify unhealthy and negative behaviors and replace them with healthy and positive ones. Patients learn to recognize why they used cocaine in the first place. It also teaches them to avoid the drug, and to cope with other emotional issues.

TEXT-DEPENDENT QUESTIONS

1. What does cocaine come from?
2. How is crack made?
3. What are some of the long-term effects of cocaine use?

RESEARCH PROJECT

Interview a substance abuse counselor, a narcotics police officer, a teacher, or local government official about the crack/cocaine problem in your town. Present your findings as a written, oral, or illustrative report.

WORDS TO UNDERSTAND

coma: a state of unconsciousness.

component: a part of something.

narcolepsy: a condition in which a person sleeps uncontrollably for brief periods.

opioids: drugs made from (or are chemically related to) opium, which is extracted from the unripe seed pods of the poppy.

Parkinson's disease: a condition that affects the nerve cells in the brain that produces dopamine.

psychosis: a psychiatric disorder in which a person loses contact with reality.

CHAPTER FOUR

AMPHETAMINES AND OTHER STIMULANTS

More than 50 years ago, Jim Bouton was an up-and-coming pitcher with the New York Yankees. He was also an aspiring writer, later penning one of the most popular sports books ever—*Ball Four*.

Ball Four was the first tell-all sports book. It went inside the locker room and exposed the once-hidden antics and secrets of some of baseball's greats. Bouton described in witty detail the jealousies of teammates, the physical pain they endured, the alcohol they consumed, the women they dated, and the drugs they took. Bouton also described how players used a type of stimulant called amphetamines when they needed an added jolt of energy during game time. At the time, amphetamines were called "greenies," and dozens of players used them.

Although it sounds minor now, people were shocked to learn that baseball players used to rely on stimulants to improve their performance.

"Greenies only allowed you to play up to your ability," Bouton said years later in an interview. "If you didn't get a good night's sleep, or you had a hangover, it would allow you to play up to your ability, or at least some players thought that." While this disclosure might seem mild compared to the rampant misuse of steroids that came later, Bouton's revelation was shocking at the time. Some of the biggest names in the game used them, including Willie Mays, Dave Parker, and Willie Stargell.

Years later, Hall of Fame third baseman Mike Schmidt would admit in a book of his own that amphetamines "have been around the game forever. In my day [they] were widely available in major-league clubhouses. They were obtainable with a prescription, but be under no illusion that the name on the bottle always coincided with the name of the player taking them before game time."

Amphetamines are stimulants usually prescribed by a doctor. But even when they are purchased in a pharmacy rather than on the street, chemically speaking, they are still stimulants, and very similar in nature to cocaine. Like all the other stimulants described in this book, amphetamines can be taken orally, crushed, snorted, or dissolved in water and injected. They can also be smoked.

A BRIEF HISTORY

Often called "uppers," amphetamines provide a person with a false sense of power, strength, and increased motivation. Some go by trade names such as Benzedrine, Dexedrine, and Methedrine. On the street, they are called "bennies" and "black beauties."

Amphetamines can trace their roots back to 1887, when a German chemist named Lazăr Edeleanu synthesized the drug from a chemical compound in a Chinese plant called *ma huang*, more commonly known as ephedra. The chief component of the plant was ephedrine. Yet

The plant *ephedra sinica*, or *ma huang*, used in traditional Chinese medicine.

it wouldn't be until the 1920s that doctors began prescribing amphetamines to alleviate various ailments in some people, including those suffering from lung problems. Doctors also prescribed the drugs to treat narcolepsy, a condition characterized by frequent, yet brief, bouts of deep sleep. Those addicted to opioids, such as morphine or heroin, were given amphetamines in an attempt to curb their addiction.

Amphetamines were inexpensive and readily available. Their effects were long-lasting. Those who wanted to lose weight, cure alcohol hangovers, or treat symptoms of depression took the pills. By the 1930s, people had begun to misuse the drugs as a cheap way to get high. Teens often took the strips of amphetamine out of Benzedrine inhalers and dipped them in coffee. Some chewed the strips, while others swallowed them.

By the early 1960s, the Food and Drug Administration said there were more than 200 million amphetamine pills in circulation just in the United States. Today, the current medical use of amphetamines is limited. Only one, Dexedrine, is used to treat narcolepsy. However, many other prescription stimulants are used to treat obesity, Parkinson's disease, ADHD, and other health conditions.

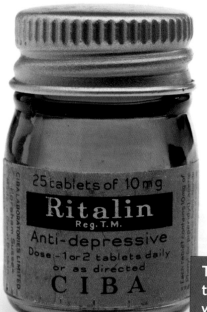

IMPACT ON THE BODY

Many people become dependent on amphetamines because the body quickly builds up a tolerance, meaning more of the drug is needed in order to achieve the same effects. Unlike cocaine, the body does not

The ADHD drug Ritalin was manufactured by the Ciba pharmaceutical company in 1954; it was originally prescribed for depression.

A STIMULANT BY ANY OTHER NAME

There are many street names for amphetamines. The most common is "speed," and "uppers." Here's a short list of some of the slang terms:

- amp
- bennie
- co-pilot
- dexies
- eye openers
- footballs
- jelly beans
- jelly babies
- wake-ups

readily break down amphetamines and eliminate them in urine. Instead, amphetamines slowly make their way through the body, causing their effects to last longer.

In the short term, amphetamine use includes a rise in body temperature, hostility, paranoia, a faster heart rate, a decrease in fatigue, and a decrease in appetite. Long-term use of the drugs causes difficulty breathing, convulsions, coma, and even death. Amphetamines can also impair a person's judgment. Athletes who misuse the drug will often continue to play while injured, which can lead to more injuries. Gymnasts, wrestlers, and ballet dancers will misuse amphetamines to reduce body weight.

PRESCRIPTION STIMULANTS

Stimulants used to treat attention-deficit hyperactivity disorder (ADHD) have become the go-to drugs for many people, especially teens who want to focus on their school work. The drugs slowly and steadily increase dopamine levels, improving the brain's ability to respond to outside signals. ADHD medications are valuable drugs, but in recent years, there has been significant misuse. Drugs such as Ritalin and Adderall help students focus their attention on their work. Students in high school and college often use the drugs so they can spend hours studying.

Sometimes dancers use stimulants in order to control their weight, but then when tolerance develops, they need more and more to maintain the same effects.

Just how many students use ADHD drugs as a study aid is not known. Some experts estimate that between 15 and 40 percent of high school students misuse the medications. In addition, a 2014 survey found that 20 percent of college students admitted to abusing prescription stimulants at least once in their lives. Among the most used are Adderall (60 percent) and Ritalin (20 percent). The illicit, nonmedical use of these ADHD stimulants among college students is second to only marijuana.

According to researchers at the University of Michigan, 5.7 percent of college students say they have misused methylphenidate, a stimulant used to treat ADHD. Moreover, a 2001 study of nearly 11,000 college students reported that 6.9 percent had misused prescription stimulants in their lifetime, while 4.1 percent admitted using them within the past year, and 2.1 percent said they misused the drugs within the past month.

Another study reported that 8.1 percent of undergraduates misused stimulants during their lifetimes, while 5.4 percent said they did so in the previous year. Still another study reported that 35.5 percent of all undergraduates in one college used prescription stimulants.

The number of prescriptions that doctors have dispensed for young people ages 10 to 19 suffering from ADHD is nearly 21 million a year. Experts say those who misuse these prescription stimulants are often under a tremendous amount of scholastic pressure. For years they are encouraged, prodded, and pushed by parents, teachers, and others to do well in school.

Students—especially those in demanding schools or programs—sometimes turn to stimulants to help them compete.

GETTING THEIR FIX

Most of those who misuse ADHD drugs acquire the pills from friends, doctors, classmates, dealers, and through the Internet. At $5 to $20 a pill, the pills are fairly inexpensive and easy to obtain. Dealers sometimes steal the drugs from loved ones, lie to get prescriptions, or sell their own medications. They then prey on high achievers, focusing on their insecurities and mounting pressure.

"These kids would get in trouble if they don't do well in school," one girl who sells drugs to her fellow students told the *New York Times*. "When people take tests, it's immediately, 'Who am I getting Adderall from?' They're always looking for it."

The Internet has made it even easier to purchase prescription stimulants. One especially troublesome aspect is that some of the pills that are bought and sold online are actually fake versions of the drugs. Not only do the knockoffs *not* work correctly, but they can often be deadly. Unfortunately, users might not know they are taking a knockoff until they notice that the effects of the medication are not what they expected.

DOES IT WORK?

Stimulants keep people awake, and they affect the part of the brain that controls concentration. But there is no scientific evidence that ADHD drugs have any long-term benefits in terms of productivity, school performance, or intelligence when they are not taken as prescribed. While it's true that people who don't have ADHD find that they can study longer when they take the drugs, it's a short term benefit. The effects only last a few hours before a person "crashes," or comes down from the drug's stimulating effects.

ADHD drugs affect the body in the same way that cocaine does. Both increase alertness and productivity. That's because the chemical composition of the drugs is similar. Both increase dopamine levels in the brain by blocking the ability of neurons to "uptake" the neurotransmitter.

Interestingly, experts say that 10 to 30 percent of cocaine addicts have ADHD. It has been theorized that these users, knowingly or unknowingly, are simply self-medicating their ADHD, replacing ADHD meds with a version of a similar chemical.

When taken correctly and under the supervision of a doctor, Ritalin and other ADHD drugs are not addictive, because the drugs take time to reach the brain, and because the drugs are addressing an underlying problem. When prescription stimulants are misused without a prescription, people can become tolerant to their effects, experience symptoms of withdrawal, and continue to seek out the stimulants even when they cause problems for them.

People who drive long distances for a living sometimes also misuse stimulants in order to stay on the road longer.

Not only is teen use of ADHD drugs on the rise, but an increasing number of adults are also taking the drugs. In 2008, 1.7 million adults were using ADHD stimulants. That number skyrocketed to 2.6 million in 2012—a 53 percent increase. Part of that rise is due to recreational use, but not all of it. For example, Paula Rudofsky was 52 when she was diagnosed with ADHD and prescribed Adderall. "We always felt that it was something for children," she told a reporter. "It's almost a relief to be told there's something you can do to help."

ADDICTION AND RECOVERY

Like other drugs, a person can become addicted to amphetamines and other prescription stimulants. Those who misuse amphetamines and other prescription stimulants will often find it hard to sleep. Their blood pressure may skyrocket. Their hearts may beat faster. They can become hostile, paranoid, and in some cases develop **psychosis** and depression.

Like other drugs, a person can build up tolerance to amphetamines or prescription stimulants in a short period, especially when the drugs are

Insomnia is a very real, and very unpleasant, side effect of stimulant misuse.

being misused. As with any drug, as a person's tolerance increases, they have to take more of the drug to feel the same effects. Moreover, it does not take much to overdose on amphetamines.

Many who become addicted to amphetamines also suffer from mental or physical problems—and in some cases these problems may be underlying issues for the addiction. When that is the case, counselors and doctors will treat both the addiction and the underlying mental or physical issues. This process can take a variety of forms, including medication, talk therapy, and the behavioral therapy models described earlier.

TEXT-DEPENDENT QUESTIONS

1. Name two slang terms for amphetamines.
2. Name three physical or mental conditions for which doctors will prescribe amphetamines.
3. How are Ritalin and cocaine similar?

RESEARCH PROJECT

Create a computer slide show or poster that shows facts about prescription stimulants and the health risks associated with them. Your project should include images, charts, and facts from your research. Present your poster or slide show to the class.

FURTHER READING

BOOKS AND ARTICLES

Braswell, Sterling R. *American Meth: A History of the Methamphetamine Epidemic in America.* New York: iUniverse, 2005.

Reding, Nick. *Methland: The Death and Life of an American Small Town.* New York: Bloomsbury, 2009.

Sheff, Nic. *Tweak: Growing Up on Methamphetamines.* New York: Atheneum, 2009.

Spillane, Joseph F. *Cocaine: From Medical Marvel to Modern Menace in the United States, 1884-1920.* Baltimore, MD: Johns Hopkins University Press, 2000.

ONLINE

Drug Free World. "The Stages of the Meth 'Experience.'" http://www.drugfreeworld.org/drugfacts/crystalmeth/the-stages-of-the-meth-experience.html.

Genetics Science Learning Center. "Ritalin and Cocaine: The Connection and the Controversy." http://learn.genetics.utah.edu/content/addiction/ritalin/.

National Institute on Drug Abuse. "NIDA for Teens: Drug Facts." https://teens.drugabuse.gov/.

National Institute on Drug Abuse. "What Is the Scope of Methamphetamine Abuse in the United States." http://www.drugabuse.gov/publications/research-reports/methamphetamine/what-scope-methamphetamine-abuse-in-united-states.

Psychology Today. "Cocaine." https://www.psychologytoday.com/conditions/cocaine.

EDUCATIONAL VIDEOS

Access these videos with your smartphone or use the URLs below to find them online.

"Why Do We Snort Things?," D News (a YouTube channel about "mind-bending" facts). "When people do certain drugs, they snort them. Why do humans snort things?" https://youtu.be/6AtYZDTrbig

"The Gangs That Inherited Pablo Escobar's Drug Empire," VICE News. "VICE News travelled to Medellin to meet gang members—along with top cartel leaders and assassins— who revealed the inner workings of the city's modern-day cocaine industry." https://youtu.be/c1EHm2_CNkM

"How the Brain Responds to Cocaine." National Institute on Drug Abuse. "Learn about brain reward system and biochemical processes that occur during cocaine use." https://youtu.be/yeAN26kJuTQ

"InsideDope: Speed and Teen Addiction," PowerSurge Videos. "Amphetamines—speed—are the third-most abused drug among teens." https://youtu.be/KHYOaTLX1J8

"Meth and Adderall are the Same Drug and Other Drug Facts." Dr. Carl Hart, Associate Professor of Psychology at Columbia University. Interview on MSNBC. https://youtu.be/zhdqhlIm4cQ

SERIES GLOSSARY

abstention: actively choosing to not do something.

acute: something that is intense but lasts a short time.

alienation: a sense of isolation or detachment from a larger group.

alleviate: to lessen or relieve.

binge: doing something to excess.

carcinogenic: something that causes cancer.

chronic: ongoing or recurring.

cognitive: having to do with thought.

compulsion: a desire that is very hard or even impossible to resist.

controlled substance: a drug that is regulated by the government.

coping mechanism: a behavior a person learns or develops in order to manage stress.

craving: a very strong desire for something.

decriminalized: something that is not technically legal but is no longer subject to prosecution.

depressant: a substance that slows particular bodily functions.

detoxify: to remove toxic substances (such as drugs or alcohol) from the body.

ecosystem: a community of living things interacting with their environment.

environment: one's physical, cultural, and social surroundings.

genes: units of inheritance that are passed from parent to child and contain information about specific traits and characteristics.

hallucinate: seeing things that aren't there.

hyperconscious: to be intensely aware of something.

illicit: illegal; forbidden by law or cultural custom.

inhibit: to limit or hold back.

interfamilial: between and among members of a family.

metabolize: the ability of a living organism to chemically change compounds.

neurotransmitter: a chemical substance in the brain.

paraphernalia: the equipment used for producing or ingesting drugs, such as pipes or syringes.

physiological: relating to the way an organism functions.

placebo: a medication that has no physical effect and is used to test whether new drugs actually work.

predisposition: to be more inclined or likely to do something.

prohibition: when something is forbidden by law.

recidivism: a falling back into past behaviors, especially criminal ones.

recreation: something done for fun or enjoyment.

risk factors: behaviors, traits, or influences that make a person vulnerable to something.

sobriety: the state of refraining from alcohol or drugs.

social learning: a way that people learn behaviors by watching other people.

stimulant: a class of drug that speeds up bodily functions.

stressor: any event, thought, experience, or biological or chemical function that causes a person to feel stress.

synthetic: made by people, often to replicate something that occurs in nature.

tolerance: the state of needing more of a particular substance to achieve the same effect.

traffic: to illegally transport people, drugs, or weapons to sell throughout the world.

withdrawal: the physical and psychological effects that occur when a person with a use disorder suddenly stops using substances.

INDEX

ABOUT THE AUTHOR

John Perritano is an award-winning journalist, writer, and editor from Southbury CT., who has written numerous articles and books on a variety of subjects including science, sports, history, and culture for such publishers as Mason Crest, National Geographic, Scholastic and Time/Life. His articles have appeared on Discovery.com, Popular Mechanics.com and other magazines and Web sites. He holds a Master's Degree in American History from Western Connecticut State University.

ABOUT THE ADVISOR

Sara Becker, Ph.D. is a clinical researcher and licensed clinical psychologist specializing in the treatment of adolescents with substance use disorders. She is an Assistant Professor (Research) in the Center for Alcohol and Addictions Studies at the Brown School of Public Health and the Evaluation Director of the New England Addiction Technology Transfer Center. Dr. Becker received her Ph.D. in Clinical Psychology from Duke University and completed her clinical residency at Harvard Medical School's McLean Hospital. She joined the Center for Alcohol and Addictions Studies as a postdoctoral fellow and transitioned to the faculty in 2011. Dr. Becker directs a program of research funded by the National Institute on Drug Abuse that explores novel ways to improve the treatment of adolescents with substance use disorders. She has authored over 30 peer-reviewed publications and book chapters and serves on the Editorial Board of the *Journal of Substance Abuse Treatment*.

PHOTO CREDITS

Photos are for illustrative purposes only; individuals depicted are models.
Cover Photo: Shutterstock/photopixel
iStock.com: 7 PeopleImages; 12 Highwaystarz-Photography; 14 mediaphotos; 15 PeopleImages; 16 PIKSEL; 24 miroslav_1; 32 Mihajlo Maricic; 38 Rafal Cichawa; 52 Marcocappalunga; 53 AVTG; 55 shotbydave; 56 YinYang
Pixabay: 36 skeeze
Shutterstock: 41 joshya; 48 Aspen Photo
Wellcome Library, London: 39; 50
Wikimedia Commons: 18 Connie Gawrelli; 23 Radspunk; 26 United States Drug Enforcement Administration; 29 Mikael Häggström; 31 Bill Whittaker; 37 Agencia Brasil; 43 U.S. Navy; 49 alexlomas